Wake Up!
Your Life is in Session
100 Insights to Upgrade Your Awareness

Kater Leatherman

Cover designed and created by
Kater Leatherman

Author photograph on the back
by Kathleen Conroy

Formatting by Candace Nikiforou

Kiwi Publishing
First printing, October 2019

ISBN: 978-0-9786136-5-5

Note: This book is written as a source of inspiration,
not a substitute for professional advice.

Also by Kater Leatherman

THE LIBERATED BABY BOOMER
Making S P A C E for Life

MAKING PEACE WITH YOUR STUFF
Say Yes to Less!

THE PAPER DIET
What You Gain by Reducing Excess Paper

**MESSAGES FOR
MINDFUL LIVING**

Kater can be reached by email at
katerleatherman@gmail.com

www.katerleatherman.com

*There is something in you
that the world needs.*

Introduction

Scorpios, one of three astrological water signs, are destined to transform. One of our personality traits is the need to dive deep. In other words, bringing hidden treasures to light brings us great joy.

And so this book. While it is written in a condensed "less is more" style, applying some of the insights will take time. Information opens the door to self-discovery but it's not enough to affect change. We must take the necessary action steps to awaken it within ourselves.

You might choose to read a message first thing in the morning and then contemplate it as an object of your meditation. As you move out into the day, the Universe - if you ask - will present you with an opportunity to put it into practice. Rereading the same message before bedtime will strengthen your resolve.

Words are energy and finding ones that speak to us is profoundly important. Language that resonates also forms strong connections between reader and writer. If my words do that for you, then I have achieved my intention to inspire the one truly amazing life that is yours!

Kater Leatherman

Unless otherwise noted, all quotes are either by the author or anonymous.

Contents

Acronyms

A. C. T.
Action changes things

A. W. A. Y.
Awareness without attaching yourself

D. E. T. A. C. H.
Don't even think about changing her/him

F. O. C. U. S.
Follow one course until successful

L. I. F. E.
Live it fully everyday

L. O. V. E.
Let others voluntarily evolve

P. E. A. C. E.
Practicing ease and calm everyday

R. E. S. T.
Relax effortlessly, simply trust

W. I. T.
Whatever it takes

Y. O. G. A.
Your ongoing growth adventure

A. J. Muste

How does one fathom a person who stands in front of the White House, night after night, holding a candle?

What would motivate someone to do this?

Meet A. J. Muste, a leading nonviolent social activist in the 1960's who was vehemently opposed to the Vietnam War.

One cold, rainy night as he stood alone with his candle, Muste was asked by a reporter if he really thought that what he was doing would change the policies of the country.

"Oh," Muste replied, "I don't do it to change the country. I do it so the country doesn't change me."

Now, sit up and take notice! This is a man who understood that his anger, frustration and resentment over the Vietnam War would have escalated to the point that he would have become unrecognizable, even to himself.

Funny how everyone thinks of changing the world, but few people think or want to change themselves.

Anger

Anger doesn't have to be the enemy
when you remember there's a choice.

You can remain at war with yourself,
brooding over your anger in a magnified
way that will grow into retaliation,
resentment and regret...

or...

you can pull back and take the time to
identify the root cause. Usually, it means
that **something isn't going your way.**

Get to the truth and you have taken
the first step toward resolving it.

Unresolved anger attaches itself to
compulsive ways of coping - drugs,
alcohol, work, shopping, overeating...
even wanting to take it out on others.
Ignoring anger weakens the spirit, so
it's important to examine your fixations.

Bear in mind that positive things cannot
happen when you are angry and holding
anger in your mind serves no one,
especially you.

Another Excuse

Excuses are really lies we tell ourselves so it doesn't have to be our fault.

If you are late for something and it was the result of heavy traffic, you would give an explanation. Explanations are factual; they are based on truth and circumstances beyond your control.

Excuses are within your control. If you were late because you didn't allow enough time, then an excuse will exonerate you from blame.

People can feel the difference and, if you value your self-esteem and respect others, catch yourself before making an excuse.

It is better to offer no excuse than a bad one.

Anticipation

Do you anticipate or avoid? Anticipation is defined as the ability to manage certainty and the foreseen challenges that come with it.

For the three things that we cannot avoid - **pain, taxes,** and **aging** - anticipation is a wondrous thing.

Pain and suffering are inevitable, but moving through it is better handled when we have put the time and effort in building a strong spiritual foundation and a network of supportive people.

Paying your **taxes** on time often depends on living within your means. Avoid financial problems by keeping an emergency fund for unexpected expenses. Sooner rather than later, determine what you will need for retirement.

Ways to get in front of **aging** are getting your Will drawn up, downsizing your living space, practicing preventive health, and maintaining positive connections.

It's all about choosing to prepare while you still can.

"He who matures early lives in anticipation."
- Theodor Adomo

Asking

Ask the Universe for something,
and one of three things will happen:

1. You will get what you want.

2. You will get what you want,
    but not now.

3. You won't get what you want,
    but you will get something
    more suitable.

*But seriously, how do I get one million dollars
and a flat stomach by tomorrow?*

Attachment vs. Love

Have you ever met someone you were very attracted to, then exaggerated their qualities? You start by bending the rules and ignoring the red flags. You might do this with the idea that the person will be the source of your happiness.

Beware! An attachment like this has addictive qualities. With it comes a level of excitement like none other, so you keep longing to be with that person because it feels intoxicating. Sometimes, the adrenaline is so intense that you have no appetite or can't sleep.

After a while, your expectations seem to be exceeding who that person is and what they can give you. When you are attached in this way, you always want more than what's there. Disappointment follows.

Love and attachment are opposites. Attachment is the need for someone to fill a void in your life. Love is the ability to cherish another person because their happiness is important to you.

Following your attachments is like sea water. The more you drink, the saltier it gets.

Back to Basics

Eight signs that you're doing okay today:

You have food.

You're breathing.

Someone loves you.

You are able to smile.

You are inherently good.

You have clothes to wear.

You have clean drinking water.

You have a roof over your head.

Life may not be what you want,
but it's what you've got.

Be

Be still and know that I am within you.

Be still and know that I am.

Be still and know.

Be still.

Be.

"Be you; the world will adjust." - Barry Popik

Boat People

If you had to leave your worldly
possessions behind and spend the
rest of your life on a boat, who are
the people you would take on board?

Who are the people that are so
important that they trump
everything else?

They are the ones who delight in
your presence, who see and hear you,
and who give you back to yourself with
love, acceptance and understanding.

Once you realize who they are, take
every opportunity to let them know
how much they mean to you.

*Any relationship is defined
by the person who wants it the least.*

Boredom

Boredom has fallen out of favor.

With the volume and variety of information available, every waking moment can be a source of stimulation. But the more external stimuli we pursue, the more it feeds our boredom.

Being bored does have its upside. It can enrich your life by driving you to change, explore something new, and awaken the creativity within. It's also a chance to rethink your relationship with the world.

There are two distinct personality types who get bored. The first group are people who don't venture out of their comfort zone because they see the world through the lens of fear. The second group feel chronically understimulated by the world so, for them, whatever is happening is never enough.

One antidote to boredom is contemplating this question: **How can I indulge a desire for change to come into my life?**

"Boredom flourishes, too, when you feel safe. It's a symptom of security." - Eugene Lonesco

Building Good Karma

Eventually, karma comes calling. Karma states that what you do in the present influences your future. In other words, you reap what you sow.

Negative karma creates the conditions for suffering while positive karma creates just the opposite - happiness.

Having good karma doesn't mean that you won't experience life's ups and downs. But, you will, according to Wayne Dyer, "seem to get out from under misfortune virtually unscathed."

Here are five ways to create good karma:

1. Have the intention to be the best version of yourself.

2. Meditate; we're more patient and kinder when we do.

3. Keep a clear s p a c e in your head and heart by staying positive, compassionate, and empathetic.

4. Honesty will attract trustworthy people into your life.

5. Live a purposeful life, one that benefits you and others.

Caring for Yourself

Self care is not just important to overall well-being but essential to the quality of your future.

Don't have time for it? Then take a good hard look at who and what is draining your time and energy. This will give you the s p a c e to service your most precious asset...**you.**

So...

Move your body every day

Make your own meals

Maintain mental balance

Mind your emotions

Meditate to nourish your Spirit

The world needs more people who take care of themselves so we can light up the world!

Love yourself grandly...
for the world's sake.

Change

It's a dilemma when we abhor the one thing that is a constant, integral part of life.

Change.

So, why the resistance? Is it insecurity? Loss of control? Not knowing? Or, do we assume that something awful is going to happen?

Would it make a difference if you could trust that something better was on the way?

Trust helps us to balance fear, the biggest resistance to change.

Do not be afraid. When change comes, strive to relax, have faith, and trust that something more magnificent is on your horizon!

Easy doesn't change you.

Changing Suffering

Changing suffering is a Buddhist term that means to move from one thing to another for the purpose of seeking pleasure.

The problem is that all pleasurable activities, the more we do them, eventually become just the opposite.

Five examples:

You are enjoying something delicious so you eat more and then feel uncomfortable.

Step into a hot tub after a long day of skiing and it feels heavenly; stay there too long and you are miserably overheated.

Spend too much time with someone you love and you find yourself longing for solitude.

Stay in the finest resort and, after a while, you are restless like the sea.

Bargain shop for the thrill that it offers and find that you're no happier than you were before.

One remedy to changing suffering is to see worldly pleasures at face value.

Clues

How can we deny that nature is conspiring for our highest good when she offers foods that resemble the body part that they most support?

Sliced carrots, for example, look like the human eye, enhancing them to function more smoothly.

Lycopene giving tomatoes, like the heart, are red and have four chambers.

Whole walnuts resemble the human brain. They help develop more than three dozen neuron-transmitters for brain function.

Kidney beans look like our kidneys. They heal and help to maintain their function.

Bok Choy, celery and rhubarb - long like bones - specifically target bone strength.

Figs are full of seeds and, when they grow, hang in twos. They not only increase the mobility of male sperm but also their numbers to overcome male sterility.

Avocados help to balance hormones and are shaped like the cervix and uterus. It takes exactly nine months to grow an avocado from blossom to ripened fruit.

Co-dependency

Is this you? Your self-worth and well being are dependent on what others think of you. Everyone else's feelings are more important than your own. You take on other people's problems. In other words, you're not sure where you end and the other person begins.

Poor boundaries and low self-esteem are just a few telltale signs of co-dependency. There are those who believe it to be at the heart of all addiction because it is so deeply rooted in our childhood. Some of us had parents who were unavailable or unreliable because of addiction, illness, neglect or even death. The result is that we become enmeshed with other people, often taking on the role of caring for them emotionally and mentally.

Naturally, we will repeat the same patterns in our adult relationships, often attracting people who are also unavailable. We may become addicted to mind altering substances to negotiate the painful reality of our unresolved feelings.

Breaking free from co-dependency is like removing a tattoo; it can be done but it is a painful process that takes time and sometimes leaves a scar. But recovery is possible if you want to cultivate healthy, functional relationships.

Compassionate Listening

Who among us isn't guilty of listening with the intent to reply rather than understand?

If your parents were authoritarian, you learned to cope by tuning out. You figured out that there was little advantage in listening to what other people had to said, so why bother.

Passive listening manifests in other ways, too. What we call listening involves the ego's incessant need to do something. Women, in particular, are notorious for wanting to be helpful by trying to fix other people's problems. But no one wants to be told what to do.

Compassionate listening doesn't mean that you have to agree with what someone is saying. It means that you give the other person the respect they deserve for their viewpoint, as you would want the same from them.

The beauty of compassionate listening is that it alleviates a great deal of pain and suffering in the other person. To focus your full attention so that the person feels truly heard is one of the greatest gifts you can offer another human being.

"We have two ears and one tongue so that we would listen more and talk less." - Diogenes

Contented Mind

A contented mind is a good mind to have. Your attitude is **I can take it or leave it.** This is a mind without attachment.

To oppose attachments is to give up the chronic habit of needing something other than what you have right now. This has the power to solve some of your problems, too.

A mind that is content doesn't need to feel good all the time nor it is afraid of adversity. It understands that underneath every challenge there is something to learn.

In the midst of everyday life, contentment brings balance. The mind isn't going up and down according to your circumstances.

Find contentment in this moment because this moment is your life.

"He who is contented is rich."
- Lao Tzu

Cousins

When grandparents and parents pass on - along with aunts and uncles - we realize that beyond our siblings, what's left of our extended family peers are the cousins.

Even though they share our DNA, there's not much written about our relationship with them. Yet cousins are special people, particularly the ones we like.

As kids, they were easy playmates. A cousin could double as a sibling if you were an only child. They can be more supportive and understanding than our siblings because the dynamics and history are different, yet familiar.

Cousins enjoy reminiscing because it keeps them connected to memories of their relatives. Family memorabilia can be shared, as well as weddings, funerals and, of course, those prized recipes.

As life happens, we grow up, have families of our own, and sometimes lose touch with people, including our cousins. But cousins really matter; they can be our best friends, trusted advisers, and mentors. With the foundation already laid, we have a bond with them that is hard to break.

Creating a Home Altar

A home altar? You like the idea but aren't sure what it means. Is it religious? Where do I put it? How much s p a c e is required? And, what items do I choose?

The beauty of a private altar is that it can turn an ordinary place into a spiritual focal point, one that makes up a part of your everyday life. It can rest on a bookshelf, a small table or desk, windowsill, even the corner of a room.

Items that you might consider are fresh flowers, a prism, a daily reader, candles, incense, a tarot deck, your favorite photograph, essential oils, and prayer beads. There's no need to go out and buy anything. Just look around and pull things that you love, want to display and/or that have personal meaning. If you want, rotate your treasures when the seasons change.

Your altar is a wonderful place to go within and recover your better self. Just its very presence can represent a safe harbor, produce a positive shift in perspective and inspire a deeper connection to something greater than yourself.

"An altar is like an airport where spirits take off and land." - Steven Chuks Nwaokeke

Dark Side of Wondering

How often are we left wondering because we're afraid to ask a question or we don't want to hear the truth when the answer comes?

Wondering can lead to some pretty scary places, especially when we wonder about the future. Will we have enough money, who will take care of us and what will it be like to get old?

We wonder about the past, and face another hidden monster. Maybe we did something all wrong or wonder if the direction we took was the one we were supposed to take.

Wondering about things that can't be changed are the ones we most need to protect.

For things that we can change, it's best to stop and get the facts. Then we find out, very often, that the outcome isn't as dreadful as we thought.

Daydream

It can be fun to daydream about winning the lottery and what you would do with all that money.

Make a list:

1. _____
2. _____
3. _____
4. _____
5. _____
6. _____
7. _____
8. _____
9. _____
10. _____

On a more practical note, what if the length of the list is an indication of how satisfied you are in your life today?

Declutter Your Computer Files

Cleaning out your computer files will make you feel better. It's an energetic thing that seems to happen when we declutter.

This is not much different than going through an old box of memorabilia. Computer files can also be fun to look through. It might be interesting to notice what you've chosen to keep and seeing how your life has changed.

Just like possessions that we have outgrown, emails can be dispersed. For kicks, return the best ones to the person who sent them to you in the first place. Then keep or toss the rest.

Begin to delete your downloads folders, unused programs, and any applications that you never use. Let go of stored YouTube videos and movies. Go into your photo library and get rid of duds or duplicates. Check your contact list for people who have passed away or who are no longer in your life.

Lastly, clean the screen, regularly clear your browsing history, and empty the trash at the end of the day.

Distractions

Being distracted is an effective way to avoid reality.

If our early years were chronically threatened, then we will develop a lifelong habit of escaping into the past or future in order to feel safe.

Distractions can be so powerful that we don't even realize how they are affecting us until we consciously take some time out.

Three facts about distractions:

1. Technology is one of the biggest causes of distraction today.

2. Distractions impact our mind the most because we are spending less time developing it.

3. The ability to successfully reduce distractions will depend on the strength of your desire to focus on what you are doing.

"You will never reach your destination if you stop and throw stones at every dog that barks."
- Winston Churchill

Dollars and Sense

Here are seven thoughts to help you keep a balanced, healthy perspective about money:

1. Money doesn't bring happiness, but happiness brings money.

2. Usually, it's not thinking about the bucks that makes us rich, but thinking rich that generates the bucks.

3. You have to find a way to be happy now, to feel good now, to be joyful now - without the money - because that's how you'll feel with the money.

4. The best way to double your money is to fold it over and put it back in your pocket.

5. Give more value than the money you are receiving…in your job, in your business, and in all areas of your life.

6. You'll only make as much as your internal belief system allows you to accept.

7. Yesterday is a canceled check; tomorrow is a promissory note; today is the only cash you have – so spend it wisely.

Embracing Your Muse

Ah, the muse…

If you are creative, you have a muse.
Muses are sources of inspiration, the
givers of the imaginative spark.

In ancient Roman and Greek mythology,
the daughters of Zeus and Mnemosyne -
all nine of them - became the goddesses
that presided over the sciences and arts.

Muses come in various forms - movies,
nature, books, and ideas. They also
surface as people who are often playful,
fearless, compassionate, and/or assertive.

Some muses stay longer than others.
Others seem to glide in and out of your life.
A few will appear briefly, just when you
most need them.

Being in the presence of a muse is feeling
motivated, awakened and eager to share
your greatness with the world!

*"The most astonishing joy is to receive from the
muses the gift of a whole lyric." - James Broughton*

Empathy vs. Sympathy

There's a misunderstood difference between empathy and sympathy. Sympathy is sharing your feelings as they relate to you. Empathy is understanding the feelings of the other person in a way that acknowledges their pain.

Examples:

If you lose your best friend to cancer, a sympathetic response would be, **"I am sorry you lost your best friend."**

An empathic response would be, **"It must be devastating to lose your best friend."**

If you've accidentally sideswiped your car and weren't hurt but mad about the costly repair, a sympathetic response would be, **"Well, at least you didn't hit someone."**

An empathic response would be, **"That's a real bummer but I'm glad you're okay."**

When someone is crying, sympathy is giving them a hug because you want them to feel better. Empathy is letting them feel their pain so that they can move through it and heal.

Environmental Respect

What are you doing for the environment?

You don't have to do something monumental to move the world a little bit. Sometimes, more people doing little things has a greater impact.

If you aren't convinced that you can make a difference, consider the condition of our planet if no one...

> recycled
> bought local
> picked up litter
> conserved water
> shopped virtually
> combined errands
> brought their own bag(s)
> drove a fuel efficient car
> used reusable water bottles
> eliminated meat from their diet

Respecting the environment is an inner attitude that may require integrating new habits into your daily round. It doesn't matter what you do as long as you do something. Then do a little extra for those who can't...or who don't care.

You wouldn't want to urinate in one end of the pool and drink out of the other.

Family Drama

You can love your family and, at the same time, dread the drama that accompanies them. Causes include the presence of drugs and alcohol, old resentments, differences, and fighting over money and possessions. Illness, weddings and funerals can also turn the volume up on family dynamics.

Every family has their tempest in a teapot. There are different personalities. Shared history heightens trigger reactions. Then there's the one who creates the most drama, usually the person who wants to be the center of attention.

Here are three things you can do to deflect the drama:

1. When a contentious subject comes up, simply say, **"Let's not spoil the mood."**

2. If someone says something to you that is derogatory, say, **"This doesn't feel good,"** or **"If you're trying to make me feel good, it isn't working."**

3. For holidays and other gatherings, bring someone outside of the family; it works wonders!

Feeling Blue?

When you're in the trenches, here are some one-liners to help turn your day around:

- Pain has no mercy.
- Everything is temporary.
- It's okay to not be okay as long as you are not giving up.
- There's always a silver lining.
- Scared is what you are feeling but brave is what you are doing.
- Breakdowns are breakthroughs.
- You are human first and foremost.
- Whenever you don't know what to do, say "I'll know soon."
- Be patient; everything will fall into place.
- There are others going through what you are.
- So far, you've survived 100% of your worst days.
- Sometimes, our lives contract before they expand.
- Life is not always an exciting or wonderful journey.
- Not to spoil the ending for you, but everything is going to be okay.

First Thoughts

Lost in search of peace? One culprit might be your thoughts.

Thoughts are like uninvited houseguests that can steal our peace, joy and happiness. It isn't the first thought that causes us trouble but what we choose to do with it. We can either let it pass through the mind and return to present time or follow and exaggerate it into something that causes misery.

First thoughts also have a tendency to activate obsessive/compulsive behavior, winding us up until we gotta have that new-better-bigger thing.

Of course, negative thoughts often take us down a rabbit hole. But even positive thinking can escalate into excitement over an upcoming event, grandiose idea, or perceived outcome. This leads to disappointment when things don't go according to plan.

First thoughts are the strongest and the root cause of our suffering starts with them, so watch them like a hawk.

Five Givens

No one can possibly escape author David Richo's five givens of life:

1. **Things change and end.**
   Life is circular; every ending
   brings a new beginning.

2. **Pain is a part of life.**
   There's no need to know why,
   only how you're going to deal
   with it.

3. **Things don't always go according to plan.**
   The best plan is surrendering
   to outcomes and expectations.

4. **No one is loving and loyal all the time.**
   We have no control over others;
   reserve that energy for the only thing
   you can control - yourself.

5. **Life is not always fair.**
   Let go of the illusion that everything
   should go your way.

*Life can sprout many vines, so go with the flow;
it hurts less.*

Freedom from Time

As the old saying goes, time has
a way of wasting us. So, I ask:
**"How might your day be different
if there was no time?"**

You might wake up naturally,
eat when you were hungry,
sleep when you are tired.

A day following the rhythms
of your body and nature is
really getting back to basics.

Gone would be asking, checking
or wondering what time it is.
There would be no need to hurry
to do anything or get anywhere.

Sound impossible? Maybe not.
Just for kicks, why not take one
day out of your precious life and
see what happens when you have
no idea what time it is.

"We're captive on the carousel of time."
- Joni Mitchell

Fullness of Nothing

Are you a digital hermit? Stressed from information-fatigue syndrome? Not able to shut down your technology?

If so, it will eventually shut you down.

Reclaim control of your energy and well-being by engaging in the lost art of doing nothing, i.e., no things…meaning no devises.

Venture out and enjoy the majesty of nature, turning your day from beige to technicolor by feeding your five senses.

Really notice what you are seeing.

Feel rather than hold.

Smell rather than sniff.

Listen for sounds that you might not normally hear.

Stay more connected to yourself and grow your life richer with more magical moments.

"I am losing precious days. I am degenerating into a machine for making money. I am learning nothing in this trivial world of men. I must break away and get out into the mountains to learn the news."
- John Muir

Gathering Years

There comes a time, usually just past the mid-century mark, when we wake up and realize that the past consists of more years than our future. Coming face to face with our mortality comes with a sense that we're being left in the dust, but it also encourages us to make each day count.

Now, we are more apt to stop arguing with people and let them be right. We strive to take on difficulties before they grow complicated. We understand the importance of making good choices.

No longer do we need to define ourselves by what we own. Things that sit, stand, or hang don't hold the same appeal as they once did. So, we simplify. By refusing to live a cluttered life, refusing to spend time with toxic people, refusing to worry about things we cannot change. We thrive more with less...all the way around.

Studies show that with less responsibility in our later years, we are actually happier than younger generations.

"The decades between fifty and eighty feel not like minutes, but seconds." - Grace Paley

Getting What You Want

Here are the three requirements
to attract what you want:

1. Know what you want.

2. Make choices based on what you want.

3. Stay focused on what you want.

*"The first step to getting what you want
is to have the courage
to get rid of what you don't want."*
- Zig Ziglar

Going Beyond

There are few things in life that satisfy our hearts more than someone who goes beyond what is necessary or expected.

Instead of the standard condolence note or the **I am sorry for your loss** sentiment, these people will ask you to sit down and tell them about your lost loved one.

Some know that a bunch of fresh flowers is so much easier for the host/hostess if they arrive in a vase.

Others will send a handwritten thank you note, not only because so few people take the time to do it anymore, but they know you will greatly appreciate the gesture.

For gifts that require programming, assembly or installation, these people might bear the cost of hiring someone to do it for you.

Transforming an ordinary act into something extraordinary makes the other person feel like you really value them.

"Always give 110%. It's the extra 10% that everyone remembers." - Frank Sonnenberg

Grace

Grace is an empowering presence that fills those vulnerable places inside.

Grace cannot be earned; rather it is given without us having to do anything.

So, what about about returning the favor to others?

Here are 5 ways to offer grace:

1. Forgive.

2. Take an interest in people.

3. Use kind words and gentle mannerisms.

4. Be a quiet presence for those who are having a hard time.

5. Look for ways to assist others in small, simple ways.

Grace:
undeserved, unmerited,
unearned favor.

Half-finished Projects

Half-finished projects can hang heavy. They are abandoned for any number of reasons. Ideas fall flat and fizzle. The "ongoingness" of every-day life takes precedence. We lose interest.

But sometimes, the inability to complete a project isn't so obvious. Like noticing if you tend to leave a project in a place that makes it hard to come back to.

Knowing when to take a break is crucial, too. Forcing yourself to push through your capacity to be effective only creates frustration, irritation and exhaustion.

Being stuck on a project can also show up when something doesn't feel quite right. If so, back off for a bit. This will create the s p a c e for a possible solution to present itself.

Starting a new project is a little like falling in love. After the initial excitement wears off, we realize that it was harder than we thought... which leaves us left to figure out what keeps us from moving forward.

"Many of life's failures are people who didn't realize how close they were to success when they gave up."
- Thomas A. Edison

Hallway of Life

We can't always pinpoint its exact arrival.
All we know is that a door closes and a new
one hasn't opened.

Bumping into walls, walking in circles, or
feeling out of sync is a sign that you might
be in the hallway of life.

Longing to be any place other than the hallway
is normal. This is where you will find yourself
wanting and wishing and waiting for answers.
It's a hard place to be.

Remain patient. Hallways are transition periods.
Think of the caterpillar about to transform into
a butterfly. This is you in human form.

Be in the truth of what is happening. The
hallway will sort itself out. Give up needing to
know when it will end. Just trust that it will.

In all likelihood, it will be an ordinary day
when that door opens and you finally
understand what makes being in the hallway
of life a necessary part of your spiritual journey.

Hands

Hands work well for the purpose
of getting things done.

To illustrate this point, if your right hand
gets stung by a bee, the left hand doesn't say,
"I wish it hadn't stung my dominate hand."

Instead, the left hand would immediately
pull the stinger out of the right hand.

Let your hands be a reminder that we
need to practice that same level of
cooperation amongst ourselves.

Let go of your self-centered attitude and
see where you can lend a helping hand.

"Alone we can do so little;
together we can do so much." - Helen Keller

Hold on Lightly

Some things to observe about
owning possessions:

Simplicity is refusal.

We can't be wanting and grateful
at the same time.

Living with less is an antidote to
premature aging.

Acquiring and achieving things
doesn't guarantee happiness.

The more valuable your possessions,
the more you have to protect them.

The more you cling to your stuff,
the less generous you will be with others.

Can you take pleasure from what you own
without being attached to losing it?

Chasing, grasping and owning material goods
reinforces self-centeredness.

Choose empty s p a c e over old objects that
seem drained of life and meaning.

Home Flow

If you are interested in removing obstacles that prevent energy from moving freely through your home - and your life - then why not consider the benefits of Feng Shui. Here is a condensed, simplified, overview of this ancient Asian art:

Create a front entrance that looks cheerful and welcoming - just like the first impression you want to make for yourself.

Clutter blocks energy, especially objects that are associated with negative memories.

Metaphorically speaking, neglected s p a c e s in your home can mean that you are stagnate in other areas of your life.

If you have trouble sleeping, change the placement of your bed.

Excess paper attracts negative energy, so periodically purge your piles and files.

In Feng Shui, there's a connection with kitchen clutter and financial debt.

Making your home an act of creation -
one that feels happy, balanced and harmonious -
is always a good foundation for your life.

Inner Critic

Do you have an inner critic living in your head and dragging you down?

If so, it may be one of the biggest obstacles standing in your way.

Maybe it's time for you and your mind to have a talk. In other words, your higher self talks and your mind listens.

Here's what you do. Create a "stop phrase" to interrupt the runaway train of thoughts before they get bigger and more powerful.

One example of a "stop phrase" is: **Sorry, but we're not going down that road again.**

Stop phrases are very useful because the mind is not always your friend, especially when you need it the most.

Stop listening to your mind; it can't always be counted on for the truth.

"It is the mark of an educated mind to be able to entertain a thought without accepting it."
- Aristotle

Just Like Me

Compassion comprises three simple words: **Just like me.**

It's a Buddhist term used to frame our interactions.

The idea is that every person we meet is dealing with some level of struggle in their life.

So, we remind ourselves that
> **just like me, this person has known sadness and despair**

or
> **just like me, this person wants to be happy,**

or
> **just like me, this person longs to connect.**

When we remember this, the walls come tumbling down and common ground is established.

"Instead of putting others in their place, put yourself in their place."
- Amish Proverb

Key Questions

Smart decisions start with good questions.

For possessions: **Is there someone less fortunate who could use this object?**

For people: **I can't afford to operate as if my time here is infinite, so why not reach out?**

For general decisions: **Is this choice going to complicate or simplify my life?**

For thoughts: **If I follow this thought, will it make me feel good?**

For spiritual growth: **Who am I? What am I here to do? How shall I live?**

The most useless question in the Universe is
"Why is this happening?"
A better question is
"What do I choose to do now?"

Kindness of Others

Almost everything you have comes from the kindness of others.

Even if you felt inadequately parented, it's important to remember the kindness of those who raised you. You were taught language and how to eat, drink, sit, and walk. Had you not been fed, diapered, kept warm, and soothed, you wouldn't be here. Enough was done for you so that you survived and became a competent adult.

You were protected by the kindness of others.

It's easy to overlook the many kindnesses that come with getting food to your table everyday. There's the sacrificing of animals and the gift of resources from the earth's bounty - the sun, water, sky and earth. There is the kindness of the growers, the pickers, the shippers, the people on the assembly lines in the processing plants, and to all beings who stock the shelves in the grocery store. And, how about those who prepare your meals everyday?

Much of your pleasure around food comes from the kindness of others.

Labels

Oh, how we have been conditioned to view life through the prism of labels!

The mind just loves to divide through separation, judgment and conflict. The world of duality includes fair/unjust, good/bad, beautiful/ugly, easy/hard, right/wrong, conservative/liberal, like/dislike.

Labels escalate our emotions, causing additional suffering. While they seem very real to us, labels disconnect us from the truth that **things are what they are.**

Drop the labels and you're in the presence of acceptance rather than a mind defined by the way you think something should be.

The next time you catch yourself thinking in twos, unclog the mental drain and feel the energy flow by saying to yourself, **life is what it is.**

"Labels are for filing. Labels are for clothing. Labels are not for people." - Martina Navratilova

Laughter

Laughter can release tension, lower anxiety
and improve your mood.

Here are seven quotes to make you laugh:

Never under any circumstances take a sleeping
pill and a laxative on the same night.

Hardest job ever. Working in a bubble wrap
factory. Imagine the self-control needed.

My family is temperamental...
half temper and half mental.

My favorite exercise is a cross between a lunge
and a crunch. It's called lunch.

If you think nothing is impossible,
try slamming a revolving door.

I'm not available right now, but thank you for the
call. I am making some changes in my life. Please
leave a message after the beep. If I do not return
your call, you are one of the changes.

During labor, the pain is so great that a woman
can almost imagine what a man
feels when he has a fever.

Limiting Beliefs

The only thing between you and letting go of stuff that you don't want, need or use are your limiting beliefs. Here are five limiting beliefs and five empowering beliefs.

1. Limiting belief: I might need it someday.
   Empowering belief: Keeping something that I don't want, need or use is preventing me from having what I really want.

2. Limiting belief: I paid good money for it.
   Empowering belief: Sometimes, I make a mistake and pay good money for things I don't use.

3. Limiting belief: I will lose my identity.
   Empowering belief: My identity is not defined by what I own.

4. Limiting belief: Getting rid of stuff will be overwhelming.
   Empowering belief: It won't be overwhelming if I remember to break it down.

5. Limiting belief: Someone gave it to me.
   Empowering belief: I can accept the love that was given with the gift and let the physical item go.

New belief + an action step(s) = results!

Litter

Humans are natural polluters. We eliminate body waste, generate garbage, and expel carbon dioxide. These are things we have no control over. One thing we do have control over is littering.

Some interesting facts about litter:

Cigarette butts comprise 50% of all littered items.

People are more likely to litter outside their own neighborhood.

Women use bins more than men; men litter more than women.

Older people are more likely to litter when they are alone.

Young people are more likely to litter when they are in a group.

Litter begets litter; people are more likely to litter in an area that is trash-strewed.

"To leave the world better than you found it, sometimes you have to pick up other people's trash."
- Bill Nye

Living Funeral

It's those trend-setting Baby Boomers who are changing exit strategies for death and dying. Celebrating one's life where friends and family come together to share and remember the life of another in a less formal and more positive way is nothing new. But doing it before they pass away is.

We can learn a lot about someone when people gather to tell their stories and experiences of that person. A mic can be passed for sharing. It can also be offered to the person who is dying.

Such an event might include a table of food and desserts, along with a display of photographs and mementos. Fresh flowers and live music can add a festive air to the room. Someone might even want to videotape the event for the family members or even do a group photo at the end.

In addition, why not provide a beautiful box to include appreciative notes and letters from all who attend, including those who couldn't.

Everyone can gather in a circle to sing the parting person's favorite song, making it a memorable way to bring closure to a celebration of their life.

Love Languages

Outlined beautifully by author and pastor Dr. Gary Chapman, here are the five love languages that show others how we can make them feel loved and appreciated:

1. Quality time
2. Giving gifts
3. Words of encouragement
4. Acts of service
5. Physical touch

If your love language is physical touch and the other person's is quality time, then you will compromise to indulge their preference.

Of course, we want others to love us the same way we love them but it doesn't always work out that way. Understanding and accepting different love languages makes other people feel important.

"It's not a lack of love, but a lack of friendship that makes unhappy marriages." - Friedrich Nietzsche

Mental App

Meditation can help to focus the mind, but if you want to change your mind, you need to download a "mental app" in the form of a positive, affirmation statement.

Suppose that you want to separate people from their behavior and remember that everyone is born intrinsically good. First, you'll close your eyes and focus on the breath. Then, envision your inner circle of friends and family while saying the following affirmation statement over and over: **Everyone is important and their well-being matters to me.** Once you feel that for everyone who comes to your mind...

...extend the circle to include acquaintances, employees, co-workers, and neighbors. Think of everyone in this category as important and their well-being mattering to you. When you fully feel it for everyone in this group, move on to...

...include people you dislike or who have harmed you. This is harder and takes longer but keep repeating your affirmation statement; your heart will let you know when it's installed. Finally, add everyone regardless of race, religion, opinions, political beliefs, and nationality.

Using affirmations changes the way you feel, think and see.

Mirrors

Can you imagine how our lives would be different if we were taught that everyone is our mirror?

There seems to be no problem when the qualities we most admire in others are like ours. But can you even entertain the idea that someone who acts poorly might be reflecting something back to you?

Do you tend to attract people who betray you? This may be a sign that it's time to deal with your abandonment issues.

If you think someone is pulling away, notice if you feel disconnected from yourself.

Think about this: What if the need to criticize others stems from an undeveloped part of your personality? What if you're being critical because it bothers you that your issues haven't been resolved?

We all have our character flaws. Seeing others in yourself is a ticket to self-reflect and heal. Seeing yourself in a positive light is also seeing others the same way.

More Thoughts About Thoughts

While thoughts may seem real – real in the sense that they're happening right now – they aren't necessarily the truth. If you're feeling stuck in your life, it may be that what you are believing isn't true.

Thought loops are rarely rational, realistic, or predictable. Feelings are more reliable than your thoughts as long as you don't follow them to an exaggerated state.

What makes meditation so hard is that we have to give up control of our thinking. A daily practice can put your mind in its place as the servant, not the master.

So, give up believing everything you think. An out of control mind is not a happy mind, nor is it peaceful. The mind is best used to focus on living in the present and intuiting the call of your heart.

***What is true is what is beneficial
for you to believe.***

Most Important Thing

What is the most important thing for you? Is it inspiring others? Is it love? Service? Peace? Awakening? Connection?

No one can answer this for you, although you may have been told what someone else thinks it is. It might not be the first thing that floats into your mind…or even your heart. It will come from a place way down deep - your gut. Start by looking at what you put your time and attention into.

Of course, as we go through different stages in life, our most important thing can change. Whatever it is, you'll know when you are motivated to back it up with action, when you stay focused, when you understand what you are doing and why you are doing it.

Take the time to determine your answer to this question. It is worth the effort because until you know what it is, your life doesn't really belong to you.

Perhaps the real tragedy is getting to the end of your life and realizing that what you've been focusing on wasn't really that important.

Moving?

It's hard to get a move on when you have to move, and even harder if you wait to tackle those attics, basements and/or garages. This is where postponed decisions lay dormant. Think boxes of pictures, your grown children's stuff, old paper files, memorabilia, and family history.

Some items in these home storage areas will need to be sold, shipped, dispersed, or donated. These are all time consuming tasks, and waiting won't make it any easier. In addition, arrangements for family members to come and pick up their stuff might need to be made.

Success also depends on breaking it down into small bites. Keep a daily focus. Stop when you feel tired. If something is too painful to part with, give yourself permission to keep it.

My point is this: Every decision that you make now is one less that you will have to make when you really need your mental and physical energy for the final push to move.

You can't start the next chapter in your life if you keep re-reading the last one.

Neutrality

Staying centered gets us close to something essential, something important, something worth the effort and that is the ability to sustain a happy, peaceful mind.

This is not a passive way to go through life but a daily "armor-like" practice, one that builds your resilience against temptation.

Ways to neutralize include guarding your mind because what you think is what you get.

Learn to separate people from their behavior.

To be satisfied with what you have replaces your need to accumulate more stuff and break the cycle of mindless ownership.

Practice noticing instead of judging.

To avoid reacting, one single breath can work miracles.

Accentuate the positive...as hokey as it sounds.

Rather than forcing outcomes, allow life to unfold naturally.

No One is Coming

No one is coming means
that no one is coming to save
you. If they do, you may end
up resenting them.

The bottom line is that you
are responsible for your
actions, finances, health,
and relationships.

You can draw insight from
others, read self-help books,
or get information online,
but you still have to do the
work.

Do not blame your failures
on society or others. It doesn't
change anything because it's
all up to you anyway.

*"More people would learn from their mistakes
if they weren't so busy denying them."
- The Gottman Institute*

Nostalgia

Are you nostalgic?

Nostalgia, which is an attachment to something that will never happen again, comes with an assortment of feelings. Warmth tinged with sorrow is one. Loneliness is another. It can also lift our spirits, especially when we are contemplating.

Gratitude is another feeling associated with nostalgia, particularly when we have learned from a past mistake. Unfortunately, it can leave us longing for a different outcome.

And how about the good old days? More than likely, you will find yourself - one day in the future - looking back on current time and they too will seem like the good old days. So you might as well enjoy them now.

Some days I wish I could go back in life.
Not to change anything,
but to feel a few things twice.

Not Always So

When something doesn't go
according to plan, it might
help to adopt the ancient
Buddhist teaching that
sums it up in three words:
Not always so.

We plan on a smooth ride
to our destination.
Not always so.

We expect someone to behave
the way they always have.
Not always so.

We think the shortest line in the
grocery store will move faster.
Not always so.

We expect a prescription drug to work.
Not always so.

Accept life as it presents itself,
moment to moment,
and you will suffer less.

*Sometimes, my life feels like
the test I didn't study for.*

Nourishing Your Soul

A nourished soul is an empowered soul.
With a daily devotion to your growth,
health and unconditional well being,
life can be as it was intended - joyous!

Here are six essentials:

Regular **exercise** is honoring the
sacred vessel that is your body.

Get adequate **rest** at night and take
pauses throughout the day to **relax**.

Enjoy a colorful array of **foods** that
not only nourish and energize but are
in their most whole, natural state.

Maintain an **attitude of gratitude**.

Meditate regularly; it will change
every aspect of your life.

Have some form of meaningful **work**
and/or **creative outlet**.

*"For life, we need three things only: nourishment,
love, and peace." - Debasish Mridha*

Opposites

Within us is a tempered place, a place where equanimity resides, where you are relatively unaffected by your circumstances…
whatever they may be.

A shift in perspective and you will recognize that opposites are opposing ends of the same pole. One can't exist without the other, nor is one better than the other because there are blessings in both.

Something essential is lost when we forget that some of our greatest lessons come from hardship. We also forget that good fortune always follows.

It's best to avoid fixating ourselves on opposites. One way to illustrate this is to consider the idea that elation can lead to depression. There's nothing wrong with getting excited about something, but the key is to keep the scales from tipping too far in either direction simply because the higher you go, the farther the fall.

You can't appreciate something if you've never experienced its opposite.

Our Dash

Headstones reveal date of birth and death but have you ever thought about the dash?

Author and educator Joan Erickson says that it represents your life and she wants you to make the most of it.

As long as time is on our side, we seem to put things off, forgetting that our dash will be gone in a flash!

What will it take to reach for something real from within and create the life that you want now?

Stop waiting.
You don't need a wake-up call.
Live while you can.
Make the most of your dash.

Dispel the darkness in your mind, rinse off the past, and listen to your life.

Outer vs. Inner Problems

We can have an outer problem without making it an inner problem.

How we handle our outer problems depends on how balanced we are inside.

Inner problems include our attitude, negative thoughts, and the feeling states that we generate such as impatience and frustration.

Outer problems are the weather, traffic jams, glitches in life, having to wait in long lines.

You can't always change your outer problems but you can choose to change your inner problems.

Solve your inner problems and your outer problems will fall into place.

"Your inner strength is your outer foundation."
- Allan Rufus

Outsourcing

Outsourcing is the secret weapon to making life easier. The balance comes from doing the chores that you like and delegating the rest.

Financially strapped? Hire someone to do the bathrooms and kitchen while you tackle the areas that are less strenuous such as folding laundry, dusting, or tidying up.

If cooking is a challenge, start a co-op where you team up and share meals with others.

Barter; keep it simple by exchanging services on an hour-for-hour basis.

Hire a neighborhood teen for odd jobs. It gives them work experience in addition to a good reference.

Paying a personal assistant will save you time to do the things that will grow your business and generate more income.

If you need a "home-lift", have a budget decorator come in and rearrange furniture, move wall hangings and suggest paint colors.

Patience

Patience is defined as "the capacity to accept or tolerate delay, trouble, or suffering without getting angry or upset." Considered a heavenly virtue, patience offers a way of life that gives you an advantage over others who aren't.

What initially triggers impatience is our bothersome, self-centered thoughts because we feel so put out. The trick is to see your predicament differently.

Travel delays are a great way practice patience. If the delay is the result of a mechanical problem on the aircraft, patience is realizing that an oversight could have been the cause of your demise.

Then stop to think how many moving parts there are in getting a plane off the ground on time. It's a minor miracle that things generally work as well as they do.

Empathy for the situation and those who are doing their best to get everyone to their destination plays an important role in how patient you are.

A person who masters patience masters everything else.

People

When people come and go in life, they either arrive for a purpose, stay for a while, or remain for a lifetime.

Those who arrive for a purpose seem to show up just at the right time to provide guidance, support, or bring messages of inspiration.

Anything can happen with people who stay for a while - fun, pain, reciprocal opportunities for growth, betrayal, joy and sharing life experiences.

Folks who remain for a lifetime tend to teach us the life lessons we most need to learn.

People leave us for various reasons. They may outgrow us, die, or simply need to walk away – sometimes without saying good-bye or giving an explanation.

No matter who it is, let them go. Holding on only prevents the natural flow of people to pass through your life.

I am convinced that different people awaken different beasts in us.

Perils of Bargain Shopping

Expired canned goods. Clothes with their price tags still attached. Items stockpiled around the house, some that you probably won't live long enough to use.

Dopamine, which is partly to blame, soars when we anticipate or see a bargain. Over time, this can develop into a tolerance for impulse buying, excessive shopping and overspending.

Warning signs include spending more than you can afford, hiding things and then forgetting what you bought, or not being able to walk away from a deal.

Slippery slopes include window shopping, reading catalogs and surfing the internet.

It's one thing to save money with coupons and discounts for things that are needed and useful. Quite another to buy stuff to escape reality, combat depression/anxiety, or seduce yourself into believing that things will fix you.

***A bargain ain't a bargain
unless it's something you need.***

Plateaus

Whether you are losing weight, engaged in a project, learning something new or building a house, there will be a plateau.

Plateaus can be demoralizing and frustrating. They tend to show up when you have arrived in a place where there has been little or no change after that initial burst of activity or progress.

What to remember:
The brain has a powerful need to finish what it starts. With that said, it's your thoughts that may be holding you back.

Impatience is caused by forgetting that projects are a long road from conception to completion. Avoid pushing too hard. Plateaus are designed to give you the s p a c e for rest and rejuvenation until your mind is ready to proceed again.

Anything really worth doing in our lives will always have some fear attached to it.

Present Moment

One thought is like a rip tide
that can pull us out to sea
into the past and future while
the present stands on the shore.

Life is about being here now.
There's so much to absorb,
lessons to be learned and places
to journey, so what makes us
choose to dive for cover?

Could it be an old wound,
a habit, a misguided belief
that living life "live" is unsafe?
Perhaps it was your past that
felt treacherous, but right here,
right now the sea is calm.

When a thought capsizes the present,
notice it without getting hooked.
Then return to the wave of your breath
so you can channel this
one precious moment in time.

*"The present is that elusive moment between what
no longer exists and what has not yet happened."*
- The Dalai Lama

Promises vs. Agreements

It's way too easy to say **"I promise."**

Here's the problem with promises. They are hard to keep because circumstances can change. There's also an emotional component that comes with a promise.

Agreements are factual. They are a mutual understanding between two people. With a promise, there's more risk of betraying the other person if it is broken.

Marriage vows are a good example. They seem very doable at the time but, down the road, you may not be able to keep them.

Feel the difference when you say, **"I promise"** as opposed to **"I will agree to _____ as long as the circumstances don't change."**

Life is impermanent, so it might be better to avoid promises and make agreements instead.

Oh, I'm sorry. I thought you meant what you promised...SILLY ME.

Puttering

Call it a day of desires
to do what you want
without an agenda.
Feed your senses
by turning off the phone,
playing your favorite music,
filling the air with aromatherapy
and raising the shades.
You're on speaking terms with yourself
and anything goes.
If your desire is to eat dessert for breakfast
and stay in your pajamas all day,
then do it to experience the joy of
abandoning your routine for spontaneity.
This can be a day of self-discovery
to see what shows up and to notice more.
To putter is to experience "soulitude"
and, at the end of the day, you'll feel
in your heart like someone who has left
sparkles in her wake.

*"If you can spend a perfectly useless afternoon
in a perfectly useless manner,
you have learned how to live." - Lin Yutang*

Quiet, Please

Living in a noisy world calls for turning your attention inward to the awakened silence that you are.

Once you become intentional to grow quiet, the roar of emptiness can feel chilling, especially when noise is normal in your life. But feel the void anyway; it's usually a matter of getting used to it.

Even with the ebb and flow of life, the one thing that doesn't change is our deepest nature to be silent.

Silence is a place of revelation and healing so your truth and beauty can be revealed.

Be willing to stop throughout the day to feel your being and your place in the world.

Reducing Stuff

Here are ten things to know about reducing stuff:

1. You won't want to do it.

2. It won't be easy.

3. "I might need it someday" bypasses the discomfort of having to let something go.

4. For some things, you will need to grieve the loss of what it represents.

5. Your kids probably won't want your stuff, so grieve that too.

6. Clearing 20 minutes a day is better than 8 hours all at once.

7. To keep a memory "alive", take a picture or keep one representative sample.

8. Most of the stuff that you own isn't worth the time it takes to sell it.

9. There will be things that you may never be able to part with, and that's okay.

10. What you don't disburse or can't get rid of may eventually end up in a landfill.

No one is going to stand up at your funeral and say that you had a nice couch and great shoes.

Routines

When life gets hectic and spins out of control, routines can keep us grounded.

Yes, they are often predictable, repetitive, and boring, yet when someone asked the Dalai Lama what one word he would use to describe the secret of happiness and fulfillment, his answer was "routines."

It's easy to be positive when you are engaged in your faves. But what about the ones that you don't like such as flossing your teeth? If you remind yourself that it prevents tooth decay and reduces plaque and gum disease, you have turned a dull task into something that serves a higher purpose.

Beyond getting things done, routines also mark time throughout the day. They even allow us to slip into the solace of the familiar and, most days, that is just fine.

"You'll never change your life until you change something that you do daily." - John C. Maxwell

Self-Cherishing

Social media has fostered a self-cherishing epidemic in our society.

Self-cherishing is a buddhist term for narcissism. It describes people who have an exaggerated sense of importance, who believe they are the center of the Universe, that life should go their way, and that they deserve to get what they want. The bigger issue is that it numbs them to their effect on others.

One way to neutralize self-cherishing thinking is to cultivate a mind that considers others by equalizing yourself with them. You will think about them as well as yourself. You are willing to compromise because they matter to you. This attitude trains the mind to remember that things don't always go your way.

"By living a simple life with a heart dedicated to overcoming self-cherishing, we are automatically benefiting others."
- Thubten Yeshe

Skin Care

The largest organ in the body is the skin and it "eats" everything that you put on it.

The biggest culprits for premature aging of the skin are the sun, smoking, alcohol, and improper nutrition.

To keep the skin moist from the inside out, drink water. For the outside, instead of creams that contain ingredients that you can't pronounce, try coconut oil.

Dry brush your skin before showering to release toxins, open pores, and stimulate circulation.

Refined sugar inhibits the effectiveness of collagen in your skin cells. Eat colorful fruits and vegetables to keep it looking beautiful.

The skin works hardest to repair itself while you sleep. During the day, be mindful of keeping the muscles in your face soft and relaxed.

Exercise is not only good for tightening the muscles under the skin, but it also facilitates waste removal.

Too much stress releases Cortisol, a hormone that can thin the skin.

Sleight of Mind

(n) il•lus•ion
A perception that is perceived differently from
the way it is in reality.

One of our biggest illusions is that we are
separate from others. **You are one with the
Universe.**

Illusions come from thoughts about ourselves
and others that are interpreted through the
mind from past experiences, memories and
knowledge. **The truth lies in who you are
now.**

Looking outside of ourselves to seek what we
think we don't have is forgetting something
important. **You are born with everything you
need.**

Replace the mind's eye with your true "I",
your "I am." **This where you will find the
infinite presence of your being.**

"All problems are an illusion of the mind."
- Eckhart Tolle

Small is Big

We would like to make the world
a better place, and there are unlimited
causes that we can hitch ourselves to,
but one that might be forgotten are
the small unexpected kindnesses
toward others.

It's hard to do when you're having
a lousy day, but that's exactly what will
help because making someone feel
better makes you feel better.

So…..

    smile more

    do something anonymously

    share overheard compliments

    pay someone's restaurant check

    give the parents flowers on your birthday

    shift from a what's in it for me attitude to
        how can I serve?

These are the gestures that will long be
remembered.

"With one kind gesture you can change a life.
One person at a time you can change the world.
One day at a time we can change everything."
- Steve Maraboli

Something vs. Something Else

Words have weight, so choose them wisely.

Hope vs. Trust

Hope is not a strategy; it denotes doubt. Hoping something will happen means there's a chance that it won't whereas trust is more faith driven. Feel the energetic difference when you say, "I trust that everything will work out for the best" as opposed to "I hope everything works out for the best."

Cost vs. Investment

Would you be more inclined to spend money for something that uses the word cost or investment? Cost feels like giving something up whereas investment feels like you're being supported.

Try vs. Doing

Trying is lying; you're either doing it or you aren't. Instead of saying, "I'll try to exercise three days a week," feel the power when you say, "I will exercise three days a week."

Problem vs. Challenge

Problems sound negative and deplete our energy. Challenges offer an opportunity to overcome obstacles and that feels more empowering.

Spa-Stay-Cation

If you can't afford to get away, but desperately need to drop out, find your center, and get into the zone, consider taking a few days off at home for the sole purpose of decompressing and nurturing yourself.

Think of it as a mini spa-stay-cation to restore yourself back to life. This can include a variety of things such as relaxing, eating healthy, exercising, being in nature, getting a massage, reading, doing something fun, or doing nothing.

This is not for everyone. For some, it may send them on an anxiety bender. Most of us are not used to being alone without distractions and the busyness of daily life.

It works best for those who aren't easily seduced by "to do" lists, "have to's" and the need to be accessible 24/7.

Not having to set an alarm for the next day is one of the best feelings in the world.

Stand By

Humans have two states of mind –
the thinking mind and the observing mind.

The thinking mind is the experience itself
and the observing mind is the awareness
of the experience.

If your mind is thinking, then who is
observing the mind thinking? It's your
"witness" consciousness.

The witness consciousness doesn't fuse
with your emotions nor does it grasp
onto thoughts. It simply observes
without bias, criticism, or judgment.

Keep at it and you will begin to understand
that your thoughts and emotions are only a
passing fling and not the essence of who you
are which is the awareness itself.

Sign on door reads:
Out of my mind. Back in 5 minutes.

Stools

The one thing we don't want to talk about is our poop.

And yet, their color is one of the best indicators of gastrointestinal and digestive health.

While certain medications and/or foods (think beets and spinach) can change the color of our stools, varying shades of brown are normal.

Bright red or black, tarry like stools may be a sign of upper GI tract bleeding.

Tan or yellow can indicate excess fat in the stool.

Green can be the result of food moving too quickly through the intestines.

Dull red colored stools can mean lower tract bleeding, diverticulitis, or hemorrhoids.

Gray, pale or clay-like indicate a lack of bile in the stool.

Life begins with everyone clapping when you poop, then goes downhill from there.

Sushi Bar

If you want to observe order at its finest, visit a sushi bar. There, you will find a relaxed atmosphere where chefs are quietly focused.

Orders are usually made one at a time. Fish is kept in glass refrigerated cases, the fillets lined up neatly and covered in clear plastic wrap.

When the chef is finished slicing a piece of fish, it goes back in the glass refrigerated case - even if the next order is for the same kind of fish.

Sacredness abounds as does cleanliness. Counters are wiped between orders. There appears to be no clutter, even when it's busy. It takes effort to make things look effortless.

Like a well tended sushi bar, the following principles are the same for maintaining order at home:

Stay focused...clean up after yourself... put things back...do one thing at a time.

"Teach a man to fish and you feed him for a lifetime. Unless he doesn't like sushi, then you also need to teach him how to cook." - Auren Hoffman

Sweeping

There's a mental art to sweeping, not so much in how it's done but what it represents.

Sweeping is a nice way to practice mindfulness by activating your senses, breathing voluntarily, and feeling connected to the **"here I am and it is now"** energy.

Figuratively, moving dust, dirt and debris clears out the old to make room for the new.

Find something to sweep – the front porch, your driveway, a kitchen floor – and make it a daily ritual to mentally cleanse your energy systems.

The ability to concentrate, especially in a relaxed way, enables you to do whatever you're doing more gratifying.

"A new broom sweeps clean, but the old broom knows the corners." - Proverb

Temporary vs. Reliable Happiness

In a perfect world, external conditions would make us happy all the time.

Being in your happiness, whether it's lasting or temporary, is to understand the difference between the two.

Temporary happiness comes from people, places, things, and circumstances outside of yourself. Because they are changing all the time, so is your happiness.

Drink this in: Reliable happiness depends on the ability to manage the turbulence in your mind. It also comes from making other people happy. Knowing what your life purpose is helps. All of this is much harder to attain than temporary happiness.

What if you put as much time and energy into managing your mind as you do looking outside of yourself for _____?

"If you don't know what your happiness is, look at what is making you unhappy."
- Liv Ullmann

Third Thing

Third things are the glue that binds.

Take a group where someone dies and it all falls apart. He or she was the third thing that kept the group together.

In a partnership/marriage, a third thing might include similar interests, a competitive activity, or a shared practice.

Estranged family members can find their way back as the result of third things such as a birth or death. Even a tragic event can unite a once divided community or help an entire country reconnect as it did after 9/11.

Sometimes, you can lose a third thing - a pet dies or you have to sell your home. Children who grow up and leave home usually require that their parents find a new third thing.

You can practice the concept of having a third thing with yourself, too. For example, it's beneficial to build physical and mental fitness but you also need to recognize the importance of allowing yourself to be guided by your soul.

Tolerations

Tolerations are things you put up with
that siphon energy from your life.

What are you tolerating?

Here are some examples of tolerations:

Infidelity
Dishonesty
Inefficient habits
Needing to be perfect
Disorderly living space
Slow leak in your car tire
Using a dull kitchen knife
Storing other people's stuff
Secondhand cigarette smoke
Slow draining bathroom sink
Keeping pens that are out of ink
Accepting bad tasting restaurant food
Wearing shoes that look good but hurt
Being around angry or negative people
Retail stores that don't value your business

We all poison our happiness in different ways.

Toxic People

In our earthwalk here on the planet, we will encounter toxic people.

Telltale signs of a toxic person:
- they don't apologize
- you feel defensive around them
- they suffer from a victim complex
- they are excessively negative and judgmental
- they lack concern over their impact on others

Signs that might be less obvious:
- they are a magnet for drama
- they complain about everything
- they don't like optimistic people
- they are a conversational narcissist
- they drain the energy out of the room

If you are in a toxic relationship, it's highly unlikely that the other person will change if you give more, say more and do more of what used to work.

What will change is you refusing to tolerate their bad behavior. We teach people how to treat us and if they aren't willing to meet you halfway, then it may be time to move on.

Uncertainty vs. Certainty

No person has special exemption from one of our greatest hardships - uncertainty. It is a natural phenomenon, yet we are under the illusion that our pain can be fixed by certainty.

Most of us have a general idea of how things are going to go, but we can never fully predict. We don't know when we're going to die, if someone will leave us, how the traffic or weather will play out, or even if the day will go according to plan.

Problems and glitches are merely experiences of uncertainty. Is there a remedy? If so, then pursue it by doing what you can. Otherwise, roll with it.

We so desperately want things to remain fixed and unchanging. People, places and things should stay the same, we think, especially when it suits us. When it doesn't, disappointment inevitably follows.

"The greatest certainty in life is death.
The greatest uncertainty is the time."
- Carl Sandburg

Understanding the Ego

Sometimes the ego gets a bad rap.

Yes, it can separate us from others with
its arrogant nature, self-righteous attitude,
and over identifying with achievements.
It can also be demanding and unsatisfied,
constantly requiring that we seek more of
what we don't have. This is an unruly ego.

But there's a way to balance the ego. One
example is knowing that you are good at
what you do (which benefits others) but you
also understand that this doesn't make you
better or more special than anyone else.
In this way, you are balancing the physicality
of life with your infinite nature.

We need the ego to individuate ourselves
here on Earth. Since no two people are exactly
alike, it's the ego that makes you unique.

Be sure to thank your ego
for trying to protect you.

Veggie Magic

Pound for pound, vegetables give us more nutritional value than any other food.

Because they are also alkalizing to the body, consuming them helps to offset the very acidic American diet. Sadly, it compromises our ability to digest food properly, weakens the immune system, and depletes calcium levels.

Fresh is best but some frozen vegetables have hidden benefits. Frozen spinach contains about 80% more beta carotene than fresh as do canned tomatoes which contain much higher levels of lycopene.

Generally, the brighter and darker the color of the vegetables, the more vitamins, minerals, and fiber they contain.

As much as possible, eat foods in their growing season which offer more flavor and nutritional value, help prevent disease, and improve overall vitality.

"Did you ever stop to really taste a carrot? You can't taste the beauty and energy of the earth in a Twinkie." - Astrid Alauda

Verbal Clutter

If the thought of drawers filled to capacity, disorganized closets, and endless piles of paper drain your energy, what do you think verbal clutter does when communicating with others?

Listen to yourself. Notice the amount of verbal clutter that goes into your daily conversations.

Examples of verbal clutter:

Over-apologizing

Habitual interrupting

Dominating conversations

Unable to accept a compliment graciously

Feeling the need to explain if you don't want to.

Always remember that less is more, actions speak louder than words and silence is power.

"We are a society strangling in unnecessary words, circular constructions, pompous frills and meaningless jargon." - William Zinsser

Whatever

Who doesn't need a word
to help tame our triggers,
one that serves as a
pattern interrupt from making
something even worse.

Whatever is one such word.
When you say whatever,
it isn't that you don't care.
It's that you don't wish
to compromise your serenity.

Don't take my word for it.
Try it out for yourself or
come up with your own word.

"Whatever comes, let it come.
Whatever stays, let it stay.
Whatever goes, let it go." - Mark Twain

Winning the Human Lottery

Did you know there was only a 400 trillion to 1 chance of a sperm meeting the egg that brought you into this world?

Your birthright is an endless ocean of goodness. Your original essence is love, beauty and kindness.

So, get out there and make the day of everyone you meet a little bit better.

You have already hit the lottery!

"You are not a drop in the ocean. You are the entire ocean in a drop." - Rumi

Yoga

Yoga is a journey of self-discovery.

Mentally, you are calming and understanding the mind so you can manage the fluctuations and put an end to unnecessary suffering.

Physically, you learn how to work with the discomfort, not against it, because life isn't always comfortable either.

Emotionally, you see how you handle yourself in a pose when your body can't do what you want.

Spiritually, you come to understand that you don't need to create calm but that the calm is already you in your natural state of being.

Please grant me coffee to change the things I can and yoga to accept the things I can't.

Your Chariot Awaits

Everything is born in you.
Who you are has already been
given to you so there's nothing
to earn.

You're here to manifest your
destiny and work out the
challenges along the way.
This, too, is born in you.
Whether you choose to follow
through is entirely up to you.

You're chariot is waiting.
So, get on board and enjoy
the ride of your life!

*As the Buddha said, just before slipping out of
his body and back into the Sea of Spirit,
"Make of yourself a Light."*

Thank you for supporting my work.

If you enjoyed this book,
please share it with others.

*Take every chance you get in life
because some things only happen once.*

www.ingramcontent.com/pod-product-compliance
Lightning Source LLC
Chambersburg PA
CBHW071612040426
42452CB00008B/1319